KIDS PRAYER SERIES II

KIDS PRAYER SERIES 2

Published by:
Cornerstone Publishing

A Division of Cornerstone Creativity Group LLC
Info@thecornerstonepublishers.com
www.thecornerstonepublishers.com

Author's Contact:
simi.olushola@gmail.com

DEDICATION

To my amazing children:

Toluwani, Obaloluwa, Okikioluwa, and Apataoluwa.

Soar, shine, prosper, and do great exploits for the Lord. May you be firmly rooted in Christ Jesus. I love you dearly. With tender love, hugs, and kisses.

-Mom

Contents

1

GOOD HEALTH

It was the annual health fair of RCCG, Ark of God. The Pentecostal church was going to care for at least a thousand individuals today as it had always done. Kiki and David were happy to be recruited as young doctors and their name tags had "Future MD" on it. Kiki hung around Tisha, her special friend, and David was with Larry. There were several providers and healthcare workers.

Kiki had helped her mother the previous night to put some red cherry juice in decorative blood bank pouches that her mother had

gotten from an online store. The "blood bags" were meant to create a health fair atmosphere. It was an open field event, and soon, lots of people started arriving. First, they went to get their vital signs checked before proceeding to the providers.

"What are vital signs?" David asked Ms. Lucy, the nurse who wrote the vitals down on a small paper used for that purpose.

"They are important measurements that doctors and nurses check to see if you are healthy," Ms. Lucy explained.

"What are the measurements?" David probed further.

"One of them is blood pressure, which is how hard your blood is pushing against your veins and arteries. Do you see this big armband? It is tightened against the arm and pumped. This helps to read blood pressure and will help to detect if it is high or low," Ms. Lucy said, showing David and his friend the blood pressure machine.

"Which is better, low or high?" Larry asked

"Neither is good," the nurse replied. What is good is to maintain a

normal blood pressure," Ms. Lucy clarified.

"Is it high blood pressure that is called hypertension?" David asked.

Nurse Lucy was surprised. "Yes, where did you get that from?"

"I sometimes listen to my mom talk to my grandma about taking her hypertension medication."

"Yes, it is important for your grandma to always take her medication as the doctors want her to," the nurse said.

"This looks like what my mom places on our forehead to see if we have a fever," David said, happy to recognize the thermometer. "Yes," Ms. Lucy remarked, "the thermometer is to know if someone has a fever. We check to know people's temperature with it."

Just then, Kiki and Tisha, with some other young future MDs, joined them.

Nurse Lucy continued: "This," referring to the pulse oximeter, "is to measure how much oxygen is in your blood."

Kiki interjected, "My science teacher says we breathe in oxygen and breathe out carbon dioxide. Is that the same oxygen this is measuring?"

"Yes, we need enough oxygen to keep us going. This little machine has two numbers: one for your heart rate (how fast your heart is beating) and one for your oxygen level (how well you're breathing). It's quick and painless!"

As the kids listened attentively, more future MDs joined the teaching session.

Apparently enjoying the moment, Ms. Lucy added: "We need to check our health regularly, to ensure nothing is going wrong. Specifically, our pulse rate, temperature, respiration rate, and blood pressure indicate the state of our important body functions."

Tisha raised her hand and the volunteer nurse urged her to speak.

"I see on the bulletin that you are screening for blood pressure and blood sugar. How does sugar get into the blood?"

Andrew also added, "Does the sugar we drink taste in our blood?"

"Good questions," Dr Yinkus observed. She was a clinical nursing specialist, with a Doctor of Nursing Practice (DNP) degree. "Blood sugar simply refers to the level of sugar in our blood. Every time we eat, our body breaks down most of the food into glucose, which is a type of sugar, and it releases it into our blood. Now, the level at which the blood sugar in our blood is good is from 70-100mg/dL. When it becomes high or when it is too low, it can have some damaging effects on our bodies." She showed the glucometer and how it is used to get blood. "Okay, "another of the future doctors, Daniel, spoke. "It is a great idea to do a health fair, so everyone gets to be seen, and the doctors can check our vital signs and blood sugar."

Kiki and David were happy to have learned more about health matters that day. Later that evening, as they were getting ready for bed, their dad led them in prayer: "Father, we are thankful for good health. We pray that You continue to keep us safe and sound. We ask that You maintain our blood pressure, heart rate, temperature, and blood sugar within the normal range. For those whose health is failing, we pray for divine healing. You promised to take diseases and sickness away from us if we obey You, and we promise to listen to You always. Keep us in good health, in Jesus' name."

"Amen," the rest of the family said.

Reflection

It is a blessing to be in good health. Let's be thankful for perfect health, near perfect health and even for those whose health is failing. If your health is great, be grateful to God and do regular checks to maintain it. We believe our Lord will heal those who are sick.

"...If you diligently heed the voice of the Lord your God and do what is right in His sight, give ear to His commandments and keep all His statutes, I will put none of the diseases on you which I have brought on the Egyptians. For I am the Lord who heals you." (Exodus 15:26)

2

DAILY BREAD

"Mom, why is all food referred to as 'daily bread' when sometimes it's rice, stew, or even pizza?" Kiki asked as she carried her plate from the kitchen to the dining room. It was a bright Saturday morning, and her mom had just made a large batch of Italian fried rice.

"'Bread' is often used in the Bible as a general term for food. It's

like a generic name for anything we eat," Mrs. Fash explained with a gentle smile. She was tired from preparing three large trays of Italian Fried Rice. The kitchen was filled with the sweet aroma of home-cooked food. She turned to get the chicken out of the oven to serve with the rice.

"What does 'generic' mean?" David asked from behind his mother. He had just entered the kitchen, eager for breakfast after their morning prayers.

"'Generic' is when we use a word to refer to a whole group or class of things. For example, the generic name for all of us is 'family.'"

"Oh, I see," David said thoughtfully. "So the generic name for tigers and lions is..." He paused, deep in thought, then looked at his mom, who had stopped what she was doing to give him her full attention.

"Animals?" he said hesitantly, hoping he was correct.

Mrs. Fash smiled and nodded.

"It's important to pray for our daily bread and to pray over it as well," Mrs. Fash said, addressing Kiki, who was now bringing water

to the table. She wore an apron like her mom's.

"I pray over my food at school," Kiki said.

"Me too," David added.

"That's great, kids. Keep it up. We should be thankful for our daily bread and invite our Lord Jesus to dine with us," Mrs. Fash encouraged.

"I don't say that part, Mom," David admitted. "Will Jesus eat real food?"

"No, Son. When you invite Jesus to dine with you, you're asking Him to 'come and sit with me.' He doesn't eat physical food like ours, but it's a good practice to invite Him to join us at breakfast, snacks, lunch, and dinner."

"Oh, so He'll kind of watch over us while we eat and take care of any poison in our food?"

"Yes, His presence won't allow us to eat poison, David. But why are you talking about poison?"

"Because I remember you mentioned a patient of yours who had food poisoning."

"Oh, that was some kind of stomach infection. I was reminding you to always wash your hands before you eat."

Mrs. Fash was now washing the pots in the sink. Although Elijah usually did the dishes, she felt this might be too much for him today. She knew her son would be happy when he found out she had helped. Continuing her chat with her younger children, she said, "When we pray over our daily bread, we acknowledge God and His provisions. Sometimes, even people who work hard don't have something to eat or the good health to enjoy eating."

"True, Mom, like your patients in the hospital," Kiki remarked.

"Yes, Kiki, it's sad to see those we care for unable to eat through their mouths due to no fault of their own. We must be thankful for our mouths, eyes, hands, and so on."

"Mom, I'm thankful for my mouth to eat," David said joyfully, his eyes sizing up the chicken on the table.

Mrs. Fash smiled as she continued her work. "Every part of our body is extremely important and useful. Sometimes, some people can eat but can't digest their food."

"What does 'digest' mean?" David asked.

"When the food we eat is broken down into small pieces," Kiki answered. "My science teacher taught me."

"Yes, you're correct, Kiki," Mrs. Fash affirmed.

"So, when I pray over any food, it means I'm praying over my daily bread, right?" Kiki asked.

"Correct, but make it a habit to pray over anything that will enter your mouth—water, food, snacks, and all your drinks too. Isaiah and Elijah always do that at school; their teachers commended them twice for this."

"Now I know where Isaiah and Elijah got the habit of bowing their heads and praying over their food," David said.

A few minutes later, as the family sat down to eat, Mr. Fash prayed:

"Father, we are thankful for this daily bread You have provided for us. We receive it with gratitude. We pray for those who have nothing to eat at this moment, that You provide for them. In Jesus' name, we pray."

"Amen."

Reflection

Be thankful for your daily bread. When tempted to throw food away, stop a minute and remember that it may be someone's only hope. Do not be wasteful with food, either; some have nothing to eat. Most importantly, always thank God for the provisions to eat and the ability to eat them.

"For your Father knows the things you have need of before you ask Him. In this manner, therefore, pray: Our Father in heaven, Hallowed be Your name...Give us this day our daily bread." (Matthew 6:8-11)

3

SELF-HARM

It was a beautiful, sunny morning at Jones & Hale Elementary School. The birds sang sweetly in the sky, and the flowers danced to the soothing rhythm of the autumn breeze. Kiki was excited to be back after the weeklong Thanksgiving break. She walked cheerfully to her class, eager to see her friends. At the door, she met Ms. Cece and greeted her.

"Good morning, Ms. Cece," she said with a smile.

Ms. Cece bent down to be at Kiki's eye level.

"Hello, Kiki. How was Thanksgiving?"

Kiki smiled even more. "It was awesome! We had a lot of turkey. My dad is the best turkey maker," she said proudly.

Ms. Cece smiled, recalling Kiki's dad.

Kiki joined the other students at the door, dropping her school bag in the designated spot. Suddenly, she felt the urge to use the bathroom and briskly walked to the end of the hall. Just as she was about to open the door to an empty bathroom, she noticed a trickle of bright red blood on the floor and heard soft sobs coming from another bathroom stall.

Frightened, Kiki almost ran out of the bathroom area. This was strange—very strange. But then, she gathered her courage, stepped closer to the bathroom, and knocked on the door.

Knock, knock, she tapped on the door. No answer.

She paused for a moment, then knocked again.

The door cracked open, and she saw a first-grade student with a blade against her skin. Scared and alarmed, Kiki jumped back in shock.

"Are you hurting yourself?" Kiki managed to ask.

The other girl nodded timidly. Kiki quickly looked around for a toilet roll and got some, wrapping it around the girl's hand to stop the bleeding.

"What's your name?" Kiki asked as she finished bandaging the wound.

"Cherry," the girl whispered.

Kiki gently held Cherry's hand and led her out of the bathroom. "May I have the blade?" she asked softly. Cherry nodded in agreement. Kiki carefully wrapped the blade in tissue paper, avoiding direct contact with the blood, using the hygiene skills she had learned from her mother, who was a nurse.

"I'm going to take you to Ms. Cece, my classroom teacher," Kiki assured Cherry. "She's a very nice person, and you can talk to her."

As they were about to leave the bathroom, Kiki felt a strong urge to say a prayer for her new friend. "But if I may ask, why did you cut yourself?" she inquired gently.

Cherry spoke between tears. "During the Thanksgiving break, my dad told me I was worthless and that I would never do well in life. He's a drunkard and beats my mom and me all the time. This morning, he yelled at me when I asked for a dollar for ice cream. I'm tired of this life and how my dad makes me feel."

Kiki hugged Cherry tightly. "It's going to be alright, Cherry," she said softly. "I'm so sorry for what you're going through with your dad. I guess I'm lucky to have a great dad. Can we pray together?"

The younger girl nodded.

"Father Lord, we thank You for Cherry, her dad, and her mom. We pray that You touch her daddy so he won't be mean anymore. Show Cherry more of Your love. Heal her hand and stop the bleeding. Give her Your peace and presence. Make her happy today, and let joy cover her. In Jesus' name, I pray."

"Amen," Cherry responded.

Reflection

We must show love and compassion to those who engage in self-harm. While they may feel temporary relief after harming themselves, they often experience pain and unhappiness soon after. Don't let the devil lie to you, telling you that you're hopeless, worthless, or a jerk! God loved you from the day He created you, and He still loves you now. Share your problems and sadness with God. He will surely heal you and make you whole in mind, body, and soul.

"For you were bought at a price; therefore glorify God in your body and in your spirit, which are God's." (1 Corinthians 6:20)

"For I know the thoughts that I think toward you, says the LORD, thoughts of peace and not of evil, to give you a future and a hope." (Jeremiah 29:11)

4

LOVE

Kiki was in the Signs and Wonders class, a group for ages 5-8 at her local church. She sat quietly, listening with rapt attention to her teacher. Today was special; it was the Value and Leadership class, and the topic for discussion was *CODE BLUE*.

BLUE was an acronym for:

B - Benevolence

L - Love

U - Unity

E - Excellence

Everyone had a touch of blue in their outfit and wore a blue paper band. Kiki was asked to mention a Bible character that demonstrated love. She didn't have to think too hard. "God loves us so deeply that He sent His only begotten Son, Jesus," she said, paraphrasing John 3:16. She mentioned Jesus as the Bible character of love.

"Awesome!" Ms. Grace, fondly called Ms. Gee, affirmed. "God loves us so deeply. Even before we knew Him, He showered us with His boundless love. He set the rainbow over us to remind us of His promise never to destroy the earth with a flood again. He gives us sunshine and rainfall in due season. He knows the number of hairs on our heads and has engraved us in His hands. His love for us is indeed infinite."

Tisha, another student in the class, raised her hand to ask a question.

"Why does God love us so much, even when we're sometimes naughty and don't obey Him?"

"God is a loving Father," Ms. Gee replied, smiling. "He looks beyond our mistakes because of His care for us. His love is so powerful that He sent His Son, Jesus Christ, to die for us (John 3:16)."

Another member of the Royal Priesthood class, Patrick, raised his hand and asked, "Then why is there death and hell if God loves us so dearly?"

"Death and hell were not God's original plan for man. Both came as a result of disobedience to God in the Garden of Eden."

Ms. Gee continued her explanation, and her students listened attentively.

"Oh, wow!" Tisha exclaimed when their teacher concluded the explanation.

"My mom tells me the greatest commandment is love," Kiki added.

"True," replied Ms. Gee. "1 Corinthians 13:7-8 (ESV) tells us, 'Love bears all things, believes all things, hopes all things, endures all things. Love never ends...'"

"Wow," Kiki said.

"Everyone, I want you to say: love never dies!" Ms. Gee urged.

"Love never dies!" the class chorused.

"Now, let's recap our lesson on CODE BLUE. B is for...?"

"Benevolence," the class replied excitedly.

"L is for...?"

"Love!"

"U is for...?"

"Unity!"

"And E is for...?"

"Excellence!" the class roared.

Ms. Gee beamed with delight at her lovely little angels. She was always happy to be in their midst. "Okay, let us pray," she said.

Tisha raised her hand and offered to pray, as everyone closed their eyes.

"Go on, Tisha," Ms. Gee encouraged.

"Dear God, thank You for the Value and Leadership class that we had today. Thank You for CODE BLUE, especially the lesson on love. Help us to truly love one another and care for one another every time and every day, in Jesus' name."

"Amen," everyone chorused.

Reflection

Love is the ultimate. It was love that brought Jesus down from heaven to die for mankind. Love compelled God to create you in His image. Every time you touch your nose, eyes, chest, feet, or any other part of your body, remember that it was given to you by God in His love. You are special and blessed, and His love for you is infinite.

"Beloved, let us love one another, for love is of God; and everyone who loves is born of God and knows God. He who does not love does not know God, for God is love." (1 John 4:7-8)

5

OUR TEACHERS

Mr. Fash drove the four children of the Fash family to four different schools each day—David to his preschool, Kiki to her elementary school, Elijah to his middle school, and Isaiah to his high school. He excluded them from taking the school bus so they could have ample time to pray together and discuss their activities for the day.

On this particular day, while driving, Mr. Fash noticed in his

rearview mirror that Kiki had a small cookie in her hand. Curious, he said, "Kiki, looks like you're ready for snacks so early today?"

"Actually, it's a gift for Ms. Williams" Kiki replied. She had just moved to a new class, and Williams was her class teacher.

"Oh, okay," her father responded, a little surprised.

"What's happening?" Isaiah, her oldest brother, asked. He was sitting in the front seat with Mr. Fash and was apparently interested in the conversation. He looked back at the cookie pack in Kiki's hand, which seemed a bit small for a gift.

"Today is May 4th, National Teachers' Day, and I wanted to give Williams a little present."

"I want to give Mr. Todd a gift, too," David said, reaching for the cookie pack meant for Williams.

Elijah, sitting next to David, quickly cautioned him. "No, David, you can't do that. You can't snatch the cookie pack from Kiki's hand—it's for her teacher, Ms. Brown."

"But what about Mr. Todd?" David queried.

"You should have brought a cookie pack for him too; it's too late now," Kiki said.

David was upset and about to cry.

Mr. Fash quickly intervened. "Okay, guys. First, Kiki, thank you for remembering today and for getting Williams a pack of cookies. She deserves it and much more. But here's what we'll do: Let's not give Williams these cookies. The original wrapping is torn, and they belong in the cookie jar. I see you put them in a Ziploc, but it's not okay to give her those cookies since you've already touched them."

"I washed my hands," Kiki said in defense.

"I trust you did, but let's get Williams and Mr. Todd nice gift cards for free coffee instead."

"Yes!" David said excitedly.

"And we'll also get gift cards for Isaiah's and Elijah's teachers as

well," Mr. Fash added.

"Oh, thanks, Dad," Elijah gushed.

"Yes, thank you, Dad!" Isaiah echoed. Everyone was happy.

Mr. Fash continued, "So, as soon as I drop you all off, I'll get the gift cards and bring them for each of your teachers when I pick you up. Does that sound like a deal?"

"Yes, Dad!" the children exclaimed, with Kiki's and David's voices the loudest as they were the most excited.

"Teachers are awesome," Mr. Fash emphasized. "They help shape our lives and destinies. We pray for God's blessings and grace upon their lives and the work of their hands, in Jesus' name."

"Amen," everyone replied.

It was now time for David to get off the vehicle.

Reflection

Our dear teachers pour a lot of wisdom, knowledge, and love into us, and we must be thankful to them. We must appreciate the lessons, the notes, the extra time spent to drive home the point, and the one-on-one sessions. May the blessings of the Lord be with them all.

"Therefore, I exhort first of all that supplications, prayers, intercessions, and giving of thanks be made for all men, for kings and all who are in authority... For this is good and acceptable in the sight of God our Savior." (1 Timothy 2:1-3)

6

ACADEMIC SUCCESS

Mr. Fash was in the driveway, waiting to pick up Kiki and David, who now attended the same elementary school. As soon as David spotted his dad's car, he started running towards it, yelling, "Dad, it's our prize-giving day tomorrow, and I'm getting some awards!"

Kiki shared similar news when she got into the car a few minutes later. "Dad, guess what? I'm on the honor roll and I have some awards tomorrow."

"Great," Mr. Fash said, once the kids were fully settled. "Isaiah and Elijah had their prize-giving ceremonies last week. I'm thankful to God for your academic success."

"What is academic success?" David asked.

"It's when someone is smart," Kiki hurriedly responded. "Kind of like when you get 10 out of 10 or 100 out of 100."

"You're correct, Kiki, but it goes beyond that," Mr. Fash clarified. "Awards and prizes are good, but having an excellent spirit is more important. Excelling in academics while being poor in attitude is not a good thing. Character is the strength of success. So, my definition of academic success includes getting good grades, learning important things, gaining useful skills, being happy with what you learn, never giving up, and maintaining good character."

Mr. Fash maneuvered the car out of the line and onto the street, heading to Elijah's middle school to pick him up before proceeding to Isaiah's high school.

"Dad, did you have award ceremonies when you were in pre-K?" David asked, his thoughts broad enough to believe his dad went to pre-K too.

"Not sure I had as many as you, but maybe one or two. My mom didn't keep as many records as your mum is doing now. Also, I didn't attend a pre-K back in Nigeria. Our version of pre-K was called nursery school. I think you're going to be much smarter than me," Mr. Fash said with a smile.

David grinned with excitement and raised his hands. "Yes! Then I can also do mathematics better and know all my multiplications, additions, spellings, and all my school work!"

"Yes, David," Kiki chimed in. "And guess what? Mum and Dad will be so proud of us for our academic success!"

"Yes, academic success," David tried to pronounce the phrase after his sister and did well.

"Dad, so tell us more about your nursery school education in Nigeria," Kiki urged.

"Oh, Kiki, it was fun, but different. We had no tablets, iPads, or any other technology of that sort. I didn't have my dad drop me off at school and pick me up every day like you guys have now. We used chalk and a 'slate' back then. We also used what we called an 'exercise book' to learn. Our classrooms were different, we had to be

in uniform, and our hair was always cut short; we weren't allowed any funny haircuts."

Mr. Fash smiled at the memory before continuing his narration. "It was mandatory to wear socks and be in uniform."

"Oh, wow!" David exclaimed, then added, "Dad, what are chalk and slate?"

"Writing materials," Mr. Fash replied. "The slate was a small writing board. You could write on it and erase it. The chalk was the 'pen'—a dry, hard, white, or colored item used to write on the black slate. It's way different from what you have now, so we're thankful for technology and how much life has improved."

"Was there anything like an honor roll back then, Dad?" Kiki asked.

"Oh yes, but in a different form. We had first, second, and third positions. Those were the positions recognized and celebrated, so our parents wanted us to be among the top three, but the first position was the real deal."

"Dad, what position did you usually take?" Kiki asked curiously.

"I tried, Kiki, to be among the top three and often succeeded, but there were times I didn't make it and ended up in the top five," Mr. Fash said, recalling his primary school days with gladness. "I'm happy to be celebrating both of you tomorrow as you get on the honor roll. May you continue to do well in your studies and also maintain good behavior in Jesus' name."

"Amen," Kiki and David chorused.

The next morning, during their devotion time, Mrs. Fash prayed for the family: "Father, we thank You for this beautiful day. We pray You bless the work of our hands. Bless our minds to remember all we've been taught. We pray You help our memory. Give us peace and serenity to understand all that we're being taught. We pray to make You proud in all that we lay our hands upon and to be the best You have ordained us to be, in Jesus' name."

"Amen," everyone answered.

Reflection

Academic success is beautiful. It's achieved through hard work, discipline, and prayer of faith. Work hard, study diligently, and stay focused on your studies. As Mr. Fash rightly said, good character is a great asset alongside academic success. We can also ask for wisdom to achieve great academic success.

"If any of you lacks wisdom, let him ask of God, who gives to all liberally and without reproach, and it will be given to him." (James 1:5)

7

OUR FRIENDS

How time flies! It was Kiki's 9th birthday and David's 6th birthday. Both shared the same birth month, October. David was born on the 1st, and Kiki on the 7th, so their parents organized a party for them on the 7th, which coincided with Kiki's birthday.

In preparation for the celebration, the children decided to invite their friends from school and church. Kiki, being the event planner, worked alongside her mum to make sure everything was perfect.

She chose pink, blue, and red as the theme colours—pink for herself, and red and blue for her brother.

Mrs. Fash decided to use Shenanifriends Events Centre for the party. She also ordered their cakes from Cakes N You, and everything was set for the big day. David was so excited that he could hardly sleep for days leading up to the event. Kiki, on the other hand, focused on the details with her mum, planning the goodie bags and other party provisions.

On the day of the party, everyone invited showed up, except for a family that had a late emergency. "Happy birthday, Kiki; and happy birthday, David!" said the first guest, Ms. Mannie, who came with her son, Paul. She gave Kiki and David a big hug. Soon, the party was in full swing, and Kiki and David were overjoyed to have such wonderful friends from church and school. Over thirty kids attended, and with the parents included, there were nearly fifty guests!

Shenanifriends was buzzing with activities, including arcade games, bowling, laser tag, and flip 'N' spin cars. It was so much fun! The fried chicken pizza was a hit, and the cakes were spectacular—one for Kiki and one for David. Kiki was thrilled to have her special friends around—Tisha, Joy, Tanya, Zion—the list was endless. David was equally delighted that Larry, Toni, and others were present.

"I got you this for your birthday," everyone kept saying as they came forward to present their gifts. The gift table was soon overflowing with presents. All the kids had a blast at Shenanifriends, enjoying the various play stations, while the parents gathered to socialize and safely monitor the kids.

Before long, it was time to go home. "Thank God for our birthdays," David said excitedly as they got into the car with tons of gifts. Fortunately, Mrs. Fash had driven a separate car, allowing her to transport the additional gifts home.

Throughout the drive home, David couldn't contain his joy. "Today is my happiest day!" he declared, his hands flying in the air. Isaiah and Elijah burst out laughing at their younger brother.

"Yes, because you had lots of fun and so many gifts," Isaiah, his oldest brother, said, glancing back in the minivan to look at David. He noticed that Kiki was also beaming with happiness.

"And you, Kiki, I bet it's your happiest day too, right?" Kiki nodded, smiling brightly.

"Dad," Elijah called, "you and Mum really went all out for Kiki's and David's birthdays. Thank you!" He, too, had enjoyed himself immensely, especially at the bowling area with Isaiah.

"You're welcome, Elijah," Mr. Fash replied. "You know birthdays are special in the Fash family, and we try to keep them simple yet well-celebrated. We're thankful to God for the gift of life and for making today possible."

"Dad, I loved my princess cake," Kiki said, remembering the crown that adorned her cake.

"I loved my cake too," David added. "And all the toys I got!" His eyes widened with excitement; he couldn't wait to get home and open his gifts.

"Yes, you both received so many gifts," Elijah said. "And so many friends came to celebrate with you."

Kiki and David nodded in agreement.

"Good friends are like medicine, as Mum always says," Isaiah remarked.

"Very true, Isaiah," said Mr. Fash. "We need to be thankful for good friends. The Bible talks about a friend who sticks closer than a brother in Proverbs 18:24."

"I love all my friends," Kiki said.

"Me too!" David echoed.

When they got home, they met Mrs. Fash in the parking lot. She had run some errands but managed to get home before the rest of the family. David ran to hug her as everyone made their way inside. They were sure to thank God for all the blessings of the day.

Isaiah led them in prayer: "Father, we thank You for Kiki's and David's birthday celebrations. Thank You for letting them have such a wonderful time today. We're especially grateful for all their friends who came to show them love. We pray You bless them and their parents, keep them safe, and let them also be celebrated. In Jesus' name we pray."

"Amen!" everyone said, with David's voice being the most resounding. He could hardly wait for the prayer to end so he could start unwrapping all his gifts!

Reflection

Friends are wonderful to have. Good friends are like diamonds—priceless and precious, sticking closer than some siblings. If you find a good friend, cherish them and remember to pray for them.

"And the LORD restored Job's losses when he prayed for his friends..." (Job 42:10)

8

PRIDE

"**M**om," Kiki began as they drove home from church, "we learned about God's archangel who was proud and got sent away from heaven."

"That's right, but what did he do?" Mrs. Fash feigned ignorance.

"He tried to be like God," Kiki continued.

"How dare he try a thing like that?" Elijah chimed in, mimicking his

mum's playful tone, while David looked on with curiosity.

"What's his name?" David asked.

"Lucifer," Kiki replied confidently, happy to take charge of the conversation. "But he's also known as Satan, the devil, and the deceiver."

"Oh," David responded, intrigued.

"He was very proud because God made him beautiful, and he wanted to be like God, but that can never happen!" Kiki added with conviction.

"What was the nature of his sin, Kiki?" Mrs. Fash asked.

"Pride, Mom; he was proud!" Kiki answered promptly.

"Good job, Kiki. Let me also add that he wasn't content. He wanted more because he wasn't satisfied with what he had. And yes, you're right; he was proud. That means whatever God gives us—beauty, brains, voice, talents, skills, connections, riches—everything must be used for His glory."

"So, Mom, I'll use my piano skills for His glory, right?" David eagerly chimed in, thrilled at the thought of honoring God with his music.

"Yes, Love," Mrs. Fash affirmed.

"And I'll use my craft skills for God's glory too," Kiki added excitedly.

Mrs. Fash then turned to Elijah. "What about you, Elijah?"

"I'll use my sports skills for God's glory," Elijah declared. He played football, both in defense and offence, and had been doing exceptionally well in sports.

Next was Isaiah's turn. "I'll use my sports skills for God too," he said, as he was also an athlete, specializing in basketball.

Finally, it was Mrs. Fash's turn. "I'll use my writing skills for God's glory," she said, and everyone clapped in agreement.

"Yes, it's important to give God all the glory in everything we do," Mrs. Fash continued. "We came into this world with nothing, and we will leave with nothing."

"Lucifer didn't give glory to God. He started seeing himself as equal to God and began feeling very important. That was his downfall. It's crucial to understand that he could never have taken God's position, but the mere thought of it led to his immediate removal from heaven."

"Wow, Mom, so when I think of something, God sees it?" David asked, a little apprehensive.

"Yes," Kiki answered before their mom could. "We learned that God sees our thoughts, desires, and everything in our minds, even when we don't say it. That's why the devil was kicked out of heaven."

"Well said, Kiki!" Mrs. Fash remarked. "Let's learn from what the devil did and never allow pride—whether from abilities, achievements, or privileges—to take root in our hearts."

"Yes, Mom," they all chorused.

"Now, close your eyes and pray with me," Mrs. Fash instructed. "Lord, please keep pride away from me and keep me away from pride. Destroy its root in me and keep me humble to the end. More importantly, help me to be content with all You have given me and to honor You with it, in Jesus' name." "Amen."

Reflection

Be humble with whatever you have. Life is like a vapor—here today and gone tomorrow. Make an impact in humility.

"...God resists the proud, but gives grace to the humble. Therefore, humble yourselves under the mighty hand of God, that He may exalt you in due time, casting all your care upon Him, for He cares for you." (1 Peter 5:5-7).

9

ACADEMIC INTEGRITY

It was the end of school final exams, and Kiki walked into her classroom, eager to finish 3rd grade. Feeling well-rested and prepared, she greeted Ms. Williams with a cheerful declaration, "Ms. Williams, I'm ready for the testing today."

"Oh, great, Kiki. That's good to hear," Ms. Williams replied. Then she added, "Today, we're only allowing pencils and pens on the table."

"Yes, ma'am," Kiki replied respectfully. She dropped her backpack and then returned to tell Ms. Williams something.

"I don't mind helping anyone who didn't prepare well for the testing, but I don't want to get in trouble."

Ms. Williams bent down to meet her nine-year-old pupil, who had good intentions but was about to use the wrong approach.

"Oh no, Kiki," the teacher quickly corrected. "You can't help anyone during the exam, no matter how well-intentioned you are. That's called cheating, and it's an integrity issue for you."

Kiki frowned slightly, wondering how her good intentions could be wrong.

"Okay... I just wanted everyone to pass and move on to the next grade," she responded, still surprised by her teacher's reaction.

"Yes, Kiki, that's the goal. But you see, everyone had the opportunity to be in class, listen, ask questions, take home assignments, and even have one-on-one sessions with me. All those times were opportunities to ask for help or attend tutorials, which I would have gladly provided. But now, it's testing time. We can't open our books for friends to copy or whisper answers. That's called cheating, and it will negatively affect your academic integrity, no matter how well you mean."

Kiki nodded, now understanding better. "Thank you, Ms. Williams. I'll just pray we all do well. I won't try to help anyone during the exam so that I don't cheat or face academic integrity issues."

"Great!" Ms. Williams replied, guiding Kiki to her seat.

Kiki settled in, and soon the testing began.

"I know this," Kiki smiled to herself as she looked at her test paper. "I remember that," she continued to whisper thankfully under her breath. "Yes, I'm done," she concluded and raised her hand to signify she had finished.

After lunch, the test results were announced, and Kiki had done excellently well. She was happy, knowing she had achieved 100 percent success without getting help or helping others during the exam.

When she got home, she immediately started talking to her mum.

"Mum, did you know that if you try to help your classmate during a test, it's called cheating?"

Mrs. Fash was surprised by the question but sensed that something significant had happened at school that day.

"Yes, it's called cheating," she confirmed, then added, "It seems there's more to this question. Was someone cheating at school today?"

"No, Mum. I wanted to help my friends in class, but Ms. Williams said it would affect my academic integrity and that the time to help would have been before the test, not during."

"Yes, Kiki," Mrs. Fash agreed. "Once it's testing time, it's too late to help. There's no more group study or helping each other. Doing so usually has consequences."

"That's right," Kiki said. "I just wanted to help, but now I know I can't do that during the test. Thank you, Mum."

"You're welcome, my dear."

"Guess my grades in all four subjects?" Kiki asked excitedly.

Mrs. Fash smiled. "I think it's 100 out of 100."

Kiki beamed as she showed her mother the report. Mrs. Fash hugged her daughter and, as always, took the opportunity to teach her how to pray.

"Let's pray," she said.

As Kiki closed her eyes, her mother led her in prayer: "Father, teach me integrity in all aspects—academic, financial, moral, and in all other forms. Help me not to be deceitful in any of my actions. Help me to be truthful in all my dealings with my family, friends, and at school and thank You for the excellent result for Kiki in Jesus' name. Amen."

Reflection

Academic integrity is an essential aspect of life. Do not cheat, no matter how tempting it may be. Stay prepared for all your tests, and success will follow.

"The integrity of the upright will guide them, But the perversity of the unfaithful will destroy them." (Proverbs 11:3)

10

KINDNESS

RCCG Ark of God was busy preparing for its annual "Back to School" program, and the planning committee was deep into the necessary arrangements. Considering the success of previous editions, the committee budgeted for around a thousand students this year. The event was packed with free snacks, ice cream, backpacks, and school supplies for children, along with brand-new clothes and shoes for adults.

Kiki was excited to see such a long queue of students ready to

receive their backpacks and school supplies. She noted the color themes for the different groups of students: yellow for Pre-K and kindergarten, green for elementary, red for middle school, and blue for high school. After welcoming some of the participants, she decided to spend time near the Bible giveaway section. The event was organized into various sections, including registration, snacks, water, juice, backpacks, school supplies, clothing with different sizes, shoes, home equipment, a prayer tent, and the Bible section.

Kiki observed that the tradition remained the same every year she had attended the "Back to School" event. Everyone had to register online. After registration, school kids received a wristband in the relevant color, which was marked at the point of receiving their school bags. They then moved on to the Bible section, the prayer section, the snacks and drinks section, and finally, the adult section.

Spotting her friend Tisha, Kiki decided to hang out with her. When she saw Isaiah at the registration table, she approached him with Tisha in tow.

"Isaiah, can I help with registration?" Kiki asked.

"No, Kiki, but thanks," Isaiah responded with a smile.

"I was just trying to be kind," Kiki offered.

Another adult, Ms. Rachel, overheard this and gave Kiki a pleasant look.

"Kiki, tell me more about kindness," Ms. Rachel said.

Kiki smiled shyly, a little surprised that she was being asked to define kindness publicly.

"Kindness is when you show love and care to people, whether you know them or not," she managed to say. "My dad says there's another word that means about the same thing—it's called 'benevolence'."

"That's right, Kiki, they are very similar," Ms. Rachel replied. "Benevolence is an act of kindness, while kindness is being considerate and helpful."

"Ms. Rachel, the Back-to-School event we're doing is an act of kindness because we're helping people, especially the school kids,"

"And they leave here being very happy. So, the church is doing an act of benevolence," Tisha added.

"Correct, Tisha," Ms. Rachel confirmed.

Joy soon joined Kiki and Tisha, excitedly saying, "I love my backpack! It's lilac, and I immediately thought of giving it to Kiki because I know that's her favorite color!"

Joy showed Kiki her backpack, and they both giggled.

"I thought your favorite color was pink?" Tisha asked Kiki, with a puzzled look.

"Oh!" Joy said, a little disappointed. "I brought it over so she could have mine, in case she didn't get her color of choice."

Ms. Rachel smiled as she watched the friends.

"That's another act of kindness, Joy, and I'm proud of you for thinking of your friend and offering your backpack so she could possibly exchange hers for it."

Kiki hugged her friends and said to Joy, "Thank you for being kind."

"Always ensure you're kind to one another," Ms. Rachel added. "You never know what the other person is going through."

"Yes, Ms. Rachel," they all chorused.

Before going to bed that night, Kiki recalled all the events of the day and prayed: "Thank you, Lord, for the success of today's program. Please help me to be kind to everyone around me. Let me show them the love of Christ through what I do or say. Help me to be a vessel of kindness always. In Jesus' name, I pray. Amen."

Reflection

Let us show the world the love of Christ through our consistent and persistent kindness. This should be manifested in our thoughts, words, and actions. Kindness is soothing; you never know what the other person is going through. Be kind! Kindness is powerful!

"And be kind to one another, tenderhearted, forgiving one another, even as God in Christ forgave you." (Ephesians 4:32)

www.ingramcontent.com/pod-product-compliance
Lightning Source LLC
Chambersburg PA
CBHW041124120626
46547CB00019B/2840